Famous Explorers

Henry the Navigator

Claude Hurwicz

The Rosen Publishing Group's
PowerKids Press™
New York

To Amy Hurwicz and Gregory Hurwicz

Published in 2001 by The Rosen Publishing Group, Inc.
29 East 21st Street, New York, NY 10010

Photo Credits: pp. 4, 7, 11, 16, 20 © The Granger Collection; pp. 8, 19 © Nancy Carter/North Wind Pictures; p. 12 (Lisbon image, backstaff, astrolabe) © North Wind Pictures, (globe) © SuperStock, (compass) © Victoria & Albert Museum, London/Art Resource, (quadrant) © Erich Lessing/Art Resource; p. 14 © North Wind Pictures; p. 15 (octopus, sea monster) © North Wind Pictures.

First Edition

Book Design: Maria E. Melendez and Felicity Erwin

Hurwicz, Claude.
  Henry the navigator / by Claude Hurwicz.
    p. cm. — (Famous explorers)
  Summary: A biography of Portugal's national hero whose advanced ideas on geography and navigation opened the way for Columbus and other explorers.
  ISBN 0-8239-5560-5
  1. Henry, Infante of Portugal, 1394–1460—Juvenile literature. 2. Explorers—Portugal—Juvenile literature. 3. Princes—Portugal—Juvenile literature. 4. Geography, Medieval—Juvenile literature. [1. Henry the Navigator, 1394–1460. 2. Explorers.] I. Title. II. Series.

G286.H5 H87 2000
946.9'02'092—dc21
[B]
                                                                    99-054202

Manufactured in the United States of America

Contents

PRINCE HENRY OF PORTUGAL.

CEUTA

HONI SOIT QUI MAL Y PENSE

4

Born to Help

Prince Henry was born in Portugal in 1394. Portugal is a country in Europe. Prince Henry eventually came to be known as Henry the Navigator. A **navigator** is someone who figures out which way to go when traveling. During his life, Prince Henry did a lot of important work. He helped explorers find new **routes** and make new discoveries.

Before Prince Henry earned the special title Henry the Navigator, he had a lot of work to do for his father, King John I. Portugal had been fighting with Africa for many years. Prince Henry knew that when he was old enough, he would have to help his father fight for his country.

Prince Henry the Navigator (1394–1460) helped Portugal explore many new lands.

The Christians and the Muslims

Long before Prince Henry was born, Portugal, a country whose people were mostly Christians, had been fighting armies from the **continent** of Africa. The armies of Africa were made up of people who were **Muslims**. The Muslims and the Christians had different ideas about religion and the way people should **worship**. These differences, along with each group's desire to win more land, often caused them to fight each other. At one time the Muslims from Africa fought for land in Portugal. By the time Prince Henry was born, the Portuguese had pushed the Muslims back to Africa.

Wars over religion have been fought throughout history.

Prince Henry's First Battle

In 1411, when Prince Henry was 17 years old, he told his father that Portugal should attack the Muslim city of Ceuta in Africa. He explained that Portugal would become richer if it took over this wealthy city. King John I agreed with his son.

For four years, Prince Henry worked hard to prepare his country for the attack. He made sure that the Portuguese had battleships ready for war. He and his father each took control of half of the army. On August 24, 1415, Prince Henry and King John I led the Portuguese army to victory in the **Siege** of Ceuta.

The people of Portugal were proud of the way that Prince Henry had fought for his country. He was made a knight, which was an honor given to only the bravest men.

In1415, Prince Henry and King John I attacked Ceuta.

Back to Ceuta

In 1418, the Muslims tried to take back the city of Ceuta. Once again Prince Henry sailed to the north coast of Africa with his battleships. This time there was no battle. When the Muslims saw Prince Henry coming, they ran away.

Instead of going back to Portugal, Prince Henry decided to stay in Ceuta for a while. He wanted to learn more about what lay beyond the desert surrounding Ceuta. He had heard stories about a beautiful city where the land was green, the river was gold, and the mountains overflowed with precious jewels. Prince Henry wanted to find out if these stories were true.

Much exploration resulted from stories of rich and beautiful lands. Sometimes the explorers found what they were looking for. Other times they did not.

11

A man using the backstaff.

Soleil

Fliche

Horizon

Radus ☉ visualis.

Altitudo turris.

Vmbra turris.

IX

A compass from 1617.

A man practicing with an astrolabe on land.

A quadrant.

A globe.

A School of Navigation

As soon as Prince Henry returned from Africa, he was asked to lead more armies into battle. Prince Henry was no longer interested in fighting, though. He had enjoyed seeing new places in Africa and wanted to explore further.

Prince Henry's school helped improve the tools that navigators used. The compass determined direction. The circular astrolabe and the triangular quadrant helped sailors find their position when they were in the middle of the ocean with no land in sight.

He decided to start a school of **navigation**. This school would be a place where he and others could learn about exploration. The school brought people together to share their knowledge about shipbuilding and sailing. **Astronomers** gave lessons on how to read the stars like a map. Students learned to make maps of new places so that others could return there and see the great wonders for themselves.

The backstaff, compass, astrolabe, quadrant, and globe were all instruments of navigation.

Strange Stories

At the time when Prince Henry started his school of navigation, no ship had sailed far down the west coast of Africa. Strange stories had been told about the ocean along the coast. Many people called this ocean the Sea of Darkness. Sailors told of a place where the water boiled red with blood. Others believed that if you sailed too far you would fall off the edge of the world.

Prince Henry did not believe these stories. He felt that his school prepared his explorers well for sea **voyages**.

Stories of mysterious beasts kept sailors awake at night.

15

Time to Explore

When Prince Henry felt that his students were ready, he sent them out on their first **expedition**. These young explorers were told to write down everything they saw on their trip. Before the time of Prince Henry's school, explorers did not write down what they saw. By the time they returned, they had forgotten much of what they had seen.

Prince Henry's explorers were different. They always came back with important information. Their maps showed rivers, capes, and bays. Other travelers could now visit these places and know which areas were safe. Prince Henry didn't go on any of the voyages, but he kept sending out more ships.

In 1419, one of the explorers' ships landed on an island filled with colorful birds and flowers, but no humans. The explorers were excited to return to Prince Henry and describe the new place they had found.

Sailors used the stars to help them find their way.

A Sea That Boils Red

Even though Prince Henry sent out many ships, none had sailed around Cape Bojador. Sailors feared that Cape Bojador, located in the Sea of Darkness on the northwest coast of Africa, boiled red with blood.

Finally, in 1434, Prince Henry's explorers sailed around Cape Bojador. What they saw surprised them. The sea was red! It was not blood that made it red, though. Cliffs of red rock and sand towered above the sea. As waves crashed into the cliffs, red sand flowed into the sea, turning the water as red as blood.

Prince Henry's ships had a hard time in the fierce winds at Cape Bojador. Builders at his school invented a new sailing ship called a caravel. The caravels were smaller and lighter. This made them easier to sail through heavy winds.

Caravels came in different shapes and sizes. →

An African Chieftain

O n one expedition, Prince Henry's explorers left their ship and traveled into the African desert on horseback. They came upon many people who attacked them with arrows.

After the explorers reported this news to Prince Henry, he instructed them to return to the desert. He wanted them to make friends with the people there. Instead the explorers captured 10 people and brought them to Prince Henry. One of the prisoners was an African **chieftain**. This chieftain told Prince Henry about the continent of Africa. Prince Henry listened and learned that there was more land farther south. Then he released the prisoners and sent them back home.

Prince Henry's explorers made many maps of Africa. This map is of a trading fortress on the African Gold Coast.

21

A Leader in Exploration

Prince Henry's great love for learning about new places and people helped Portugal become a leader in exploration. Many young explorers got their start at his school of navigation. Prince Henry died peacefully at his home in 1460. He had no money when he died. He had spent his entire fortune on voyages of discovery.

Henry the Navigator's Timeline

1394-Prince Henry is born in Portugal.

1415-Prince Henry and his father, King John I, conquer the Muslim city of Ceuta in Africa.

1434-Prince Henry's explorers sail around Cape Bojador and discover a blood-red sea.

1460-Henry the Navigator dies peacefully.

Glossary

astronomers (uh-STRA-nuh-merz) People who study the night sky and the planets, moons, stars, and other objects found in space.

chieftain (CHEEF-tin) A leader of a group.

continent (KON-tin-ent) One of the seven great masses of land on the earth.

expedition (EK-spuh-DIH-shun) A trip taken for a special purpose.

Muslims (MUHZ-limz) People who believe in the Islamic religion.

navigation (NAH-vuh-GAY-shun) A way of figuring out which way a ship is headed.

navigator (NA-vuh-gay-tur) An explorer of the seas.

routes (ROOTS) Paths you take to get places.

siege (SEEJ) A strong attack.

voyages (VOY-ih-jez) Journeys by water.

worship (VVUR-ship) To pay great honor or respect to something or someone.

Index

Web Sites:

To learn more about Henry the Navigator, check out these Web sites:
http://www.acs.ucalgary.ca/HIST/tutor/eurvoya/henry1.html
http://www.mrdowling.com/610-henry.html